The Big Dig

Reshaping an American City

Peter Vanderwarker

Little, Brown and Company
Boston   New York   Toronto   London

This book is for my two wonderful children, Amy and Christopher.
I love them for their adventuresome spirits and humanitarian hearts.

Acknowledgments

For his vision, toughness, and humanity: Fred Salvucci

To John Keller at Little, Brown and Company for support and good advice

For patience, dedication, and wonderful bookmaking: Vernon Press, Inc.

For encouragement and guidance over the years: Rebecca Barnes, Claire Barrett, and Robert Campbell

To the professionals at Wallace Floyd Design Group: Dave Wallace, Skip Smallridge, Peter Brigham, and Don Kindsvatter

To Paul Lukez and Todd Boyd at Lukez Architects

To the staff of the Central Artery/Tunnel Project: Terry Brown, Dan McNichol, Joe Allegro, Mike Bertoulin, Matt Seel, Al McPhail, Tony Lancelotti, Sean O'Neill, Dennis Rahilly, and Andrew Natsios

For critical research: David Luberoff, Peter Zuk, and Yanni Tsipis

For very early support of this project: Barney Adams, Mary Fifield, Claire Barrett, Peter Karoff, Bob Weinberg, and Julius Levin

For their grant in 1989: The National Endowment for the Arts

For their support and guidance since 1978: *The Boston Globe*

And for their consistent patience and humor: my wife, Richie, and my brother Tony

Picture credits: All of the images except those listed below are courtesy of Peter Vanderwarker

Courtesy of the Norman B. Leventhal Map Collection, **p. 6**; Boston Public Library/Rare Books Department. Courtesy of the Trustees, **p. 7**; Library of Congress, **p. 8 (left)**; Courtesy of the Bostonian Society/Old State House, **p. 8 (center)**; Photograph by William Litant, **p. 8 (right)**; Courtesy of the Boston Public Library, Print Department. Photograph by Leslie Jones, **p. 9 (left)**; Boston Athenaeum. Photograph by George M. Cushing Jr., **p. 9 (center)**; Thomas P. O'Neill Papers, John J. Burns Library, Boston College, **p. 13 (top)**; Courtesy Ronald Reagan Library, **p. 13 (bottom)**; Boston, Mass., State Street, circa 1903. From the Boston Transit Commission, BTC Env. #1293. Courtesy of the Society for the Preservation of New England Antiquities, **p. 15 (bottom left)**; Courtesy of Massachusetts Turnpike Authority, Central Artery/Tunnel Project, **pp. 15 (top), 16-17, 32-33**; ©Louis Martin, **p. 26**; ©Bob O'Connor, **pp. 29 (bottom), 30**; Courtesy of Dr. Robert Hasenstaub, **p. 37**; Courtesy of the Massachusetts Historical Commission, Office of the Secretary of the Commonwealth, William Francis Galvin. Paddy's Alley Site, Boston, **p. 37 (inset)**; Courtesy of Paul Lukez, **p. 42**; Courtesy of Wallace Floyd Design Group, **p. 43 (bottom)**; Courtesy of Elaine Spatz-Rabinowitz, **p. 53 (top)**; Courtesy of the Metropolitan District Commission, **p. 53 (bottom)**. Original illustrations **(pp. 23, 40, and 45 bottom)** by Howard S. Friedman.

Designed by Peter M. Blaiwas, Vernon Press Inc., Boston

First Edition

ISBN 0-316-60598-0

Library of Congress Control Number 00-111932

10 9 8 7 6 5 4 3 2 1

Printed in Hong Kong

CONTENTS

Something big is happening in Boston, Massachusetts.

Boston's Central Artery/Tunnel Project, also known as the Big Dig, is in full swing. The Big Dig is the largest and most complex construction project that any American city has ever seen. But the Big Dig is more than just a giant construction project. It is a story of vision, determination, and cooperation.

The Big Dig is an effort to solve Boston's massive traffic problems. Boston is a charming, historic place, but driving through the city has never been easy. You can walk across the city in nearly half the time it takes to drive the same distance. For years, too many automobiles have been trying to squeeze through the city's network of old and outdated roads, bridges, and tunnels, causing big traffic jams. But rather than simply fixing Boston's existing transportation network, the Big Dig is transforming it. This means building new tunnels and bridges and replacing an awful elevated highway with an underground **expressway**. When finished, the Big Dig will have taken nearly twenty years to complete, cost more than fourteen billion dollars, and permanently changed the face of Boston.

But how did traffic in Boston get so bad in the first place? And why is the city going through so much trouble to fix the problem?

A typical day on the Big Dig:
A new bridge (facing page) rises above Boston's Charles River. Behind the bridge is the Central Artery, an elevated highway that is being replaced by a tunnel underneath the city.

Meanwhile, beneath the streets of downtown Boston (above), construction workers monitor the progress of a new underground expressway.

Across the city, a welder (left) connects studs at the entrance of the Ted Williams Tunnel, which runs underneath Boston Harbor.

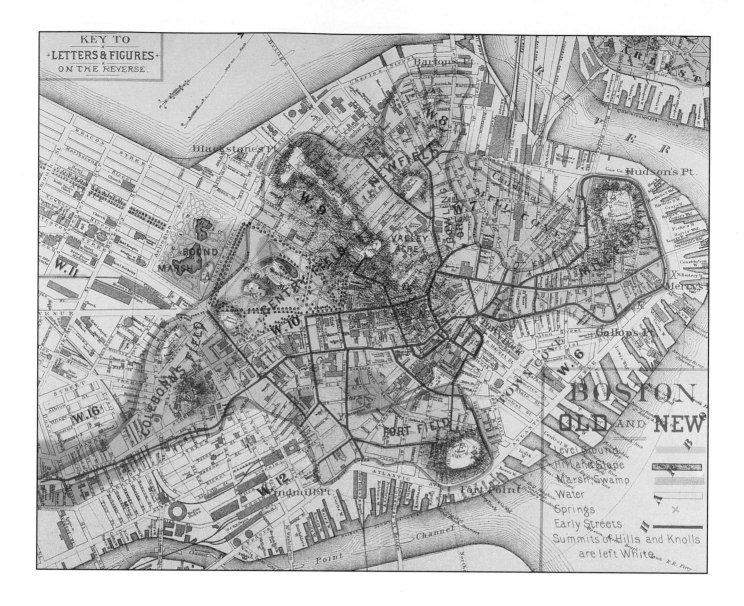

BLAME IT ON BLAXTON ■ If Reverend William Blaxton, Boston's first European settler, hadn't chosen to make his home on the Shawmut Peninsula in 1625, the Big Dig might never have happened. Blaxton loved the peninsula's tall hills, its lovely coves, and its supply of fresh spring water. The Reverend lived alone until 1630, when Governor John Winthrop and his Massachusetts Bay Colony joined him on the tiny, water-ringed **peninsula.** Boston was born, and the fight for space was on.

This map of Boston, drawn in 1880, illustrates the physical expansion of the city over two hundred and fifty years. The yellow area (bounded by the green line) shows the original outline of the Shawmut Peninsula.

In its early days, Boston's fortunes came from the sea. Ships brought goods to Boston from all parts of the world, and wharves extended from the peninsula's ample shoreline like fingers into the deep waters of Boston Harbor. Unfortunately, Boston didn't have a lot of room to accommodate its growing population. To make more land for their city, Bostonians cut away the tops of their hills and used the dirt to fill in land between the wharves. By the time America gained its independence in 1776, Boston had become a bustling town filled with homes, warehouses, and churches and criss-crossed by narrow, winding streets.

Boston continued to grow throughout the 1800s, as waves of immigrants moved to the city. The peninsula continued to expand as the city cut down more hills to fill in marshes and coves along the waterfront. Yet congestion became a problem. Boston's narrow streets were wonderful for pedestrians, but terrible for commercial traffic. In the 1870s, the streets around the waterfront were jammed with horse-drawn wagons, pedestrians, and goods waiting to be loaded onto ships tied up at the wharves. Railroad terminals and tracks were everywhere, as trains moved goods and people in and out of Boston.

Soon after European settlers arrived on the Shawmut Peninsula, Boston began reaching out to the sea. As a result, all of Boston's modern-day waterfront rests on unstable fill.

ALONG COMES THE AUTOMOBILE ■

Bostonians laughed when the first automobiles appeared around 1900. But by the 1930s, Americans were in love with the car, and people in Boston realized that the city would need bigger roads to handle the growing automobile traffic. Over the next few decades, in response to these problems, politicians and administrators planned and built a series of highways and tunnels: Storrow Drive, the Sumner and Callahan Tunnels, the Massachusetts Turnpike, and the Central Artery. These roads were built to carry traffic into, out of, and around Boston and to free up the city's crowded streets. Ribbons of highway were quickly replacing Boston's crooked streets.

The Central Artery was the most important of Boston's new roads. Engineers designed this "highway in the sky" to deliver traffic to the heart of downtown Boston and open

TRAFFIC ALERT: A Central Artery Timeline

1906 Electric streetcars and pedestrians crowd Washington Street, downtown Boston's busiest shopping area. Although Boston's narrow streets were full of character and charm, their size caused major congestion. As a result, the city was diffiicult to navigate.

1925 Cars gas up in Park Square in 1925. A report from the same year cited "intolerable conditions" in downtown Boston due to the influx of automobiles. In 1930, city officials approved a plan to build a highway through downtown to fix the problem. It would take more than thirty years for the idea to become reality.

1950s Construction begins on the Central Artery. To clear a path for the elevated highway, the city had to destroy more than a thousand homes and small businesses. Despite protests from residents, community leaders, and merchants' associations, nearly twenty thousand people were forced out of their homes and places of business.

up shopping and office jobs to the growing suburban population. The elevated highway ran right through the oldest part of Boston, connecting the city with other new roads in the south and in the north. City planners believed that the Central Artery, with its many exit and entry ramps, would enable cars and delivery trucks to get in and out of downtown quickly. Surface streets and parking spaces underneath the elevated highway would allow motorists to drive and park close to their destinations. The road was intended to work in concert with another highway, called the Inner Belt, that, when built, would enable through traffic to bypass the city.

But the Central Artery didn't turn out as planned. The highway cut a huge swath through the heart of the city, taking space and forming an ugly backdrop for some of the city's historic neighborhoods, such as

1953-1959 The elevated section of the Central Artery opened up in 1956. Realizing that an elevated highway in the middle of the city was disruptive and unattractive, city officials decided to put the last part of the road underground. When the highway was completed in 1959, it carried a fraction of its capacity of 75,000 cars per day.

1989 By the end of the 1980s, the Central Artery was carrying more than 150,000 cars per day. Traffic was bumper-to-bumper for up to eight hours each day. In addition, the accident rate on the Central Artery was more than four times the national average. Obsolete, crumbling, and dangerous, the road had turned into Boston's worst nightmare.

the North End. The road also separated downtown Boston from these neighborhoods and from the waterfront. In places, the Central Artery and its access ramps were 400 feet wide. The hulking green structure engulfed the streets and sidewalks near it with darkness, noise, and dirt. Only pigeons seemed to be happy there. Planners eventually realized what a mistake it was and put the remaining one-half mile in a tunnel under the city.

An even bigger problem was that the Central Artery was soon carrying more cars than it could handle. The city never built the Inner Belt highway, so the Central Artery wound up carrying both local and regional traffic. By the early 1970s, the Artery was over-crowded and starting to fall apart. Instead of solving Boston's traffic problems, the Central Artery had only made them worse. Everyone wanted to see the road repaired or replaced.

A map of Boston and surrounding areas (above) illustrates the number of roads that feed into the Central Artery (93). The increasing number of cars traveling into and through Boston on these roads pushed the artery beyond its capacity.

This photo (left), taken from underneath the Central Artery, shows the shadow that the road casts on the streets of Boston.

FRED SALVUCCI'S DILEMMA ■ Fred Salvucci, the secretary of transportation for the state of Massachusetts, was one of the people who wanted to see the Central Artery replaced. Salvucci, who was trained as a civil engineer, had never thought seriously about removing the Central Artery until he talked with Bill Reynolds, a **contractor** who made his living building highways. Salvucci recalls: "One day in 1971 Bill came to me and said, 'The Central Artery is ugly and it doesn't work. If we put it underground, in a beautiful tunnel, then everyone will like highways, and I will get more work.' I told Reynolds he was crazy, but I became fascinated with the idea."

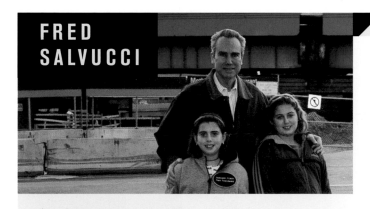

FRED
SALVUCCI

Fred Salvucci (above, with his granddaughters) is full of contradictions. He hates cars but he builds highways. He is an engineer but has the imagination of an artist. He knows details but he can see the big picture as well. He buckles his belt on the side of his hip, as they did in the 1950s, but he thinks ahead of his time. One event from 1962 stands out in his mind.

"Back then, the people building the Massachusetts Turnpike gave my grandmother a dollar for her house. A dollar in an envelope for the place a person lives. It was appalling." Like many others, Fred was bothered by the fact that the city destroyed homes and communities to build highways. To Fred, it was a crime for a highway project to take homes away from even one person.

Fred learned from this experience that cities needed to take a different approach to building highways. He decided that highway projects could work if cities addressed environmental issues and responded to the concerns of the people affected by the construction, rather than ignoring them. So, as secretary of transportation, he put aside his dislike of highways and supported the idea of putting the Central Artery underground. Believing that it could help the city if handled properly, Fred became the leading advocate for the Big Dig.

Fred realized that replacing the elevated Central Artery with a wider, underground expressway would speed traffic and remove an eyesore from the city. The idea of building a new tunnel under an existing elevated highway seemed impossible, but if nothing was done, the city would choke on its own cars.

Fred knew that Massachusetts would need a lot of money to undertake such a project. Fortunately, the Central Artery is part of the Interstate Highway System, a project begun in 1956 by the federal government to create large, controlled-access highways across the United States. Federal money was still available to finish the highway system, and the Central Artery was eligible for funding because it had been started prior to 1956 and needed to be brought up to federal highway standards. At the same time, Boston was trying to get federal funding to build a third tunnel under Boston Harbor to connect the Massachusetts **Turnpike** to Logan Airport in East Boston. Fred managed to combine the two competing projects into one proposal. He then began to organize a request for federal funding.

One of the first environmental impact studies for the project was due at the Federal Highway Administration office in Boston at 5:00 p.m. on a certain Friday in 1983. Appropriately, the submission was late because the car carrying it got stuck in a huge traffic jam.

THE FIGHT FOR FUNDING ■ Convincing federal officials to provide money for a large project took political skill, and Massachusetts was fortunate to have Congressman Thomas "Tip" O'Neill stating its case. O'Neill, a Democrat from an Irish neighborhood near Boston, and President Ronald Reagan, a Republican from a suburb in California, were on opposite sides of the Central Artery Project. Tip knew that removing the elevated highway would be a permanent gift to neighborhoods like the North End, but Reagan saw the project as a waste of federal money for small local benefit.

As Speaker of the House of Representatives, Tip O'Neill wielded great skill and power. Still, it took four years of intense political work on his part to bring the funding bill to a vote in the Senate. After two close votes, Congress overrode a veto by President Reagan and approved funding for the Central Artery in April 1987.

Once Congress had approved the funding bill, the design and planning of the Central Artery/Tunnel Project shifted into high gear. Boston would never be the same.

Tip O'Neill (top) and Ronald Reagan (above) strongly disagreed about the value and necessity of the Central Artery/Tunnel Project. As they battled, the problem only got worse. Traffic continued to inch along the Central Artery (left), creating massive traffic jams and polluting the city's air.

Coordinating the planning and design of the Central Artery/Tunnel Project was the engineering firm of Bechtel/Parsons Brinkerhoff. Their job was to figure out how to build new tunnels and bridges and connect them

with the maze of highways and streets serving the city. Performing these tasks was going to be hard enough. But an even bigger issue lay ahead. The challenge for all involved was how to do these things without shutting down the city. City and project leaders realized that you couldn't just post a sign in downtown Boston saying "Closed for business—come back in ten years." Furthermore, engineers, designers, and contractors had to find a way to fit a lot of large construction equipment into a crowded city. The project called for careful planning, perseverance, and innovative technology.

A designer works on a model for the Central Artery/Tunnel Project. Urban designers from Wallace Floyd, Associates led the effort to design dozens of miles of new tunnels and bridges.

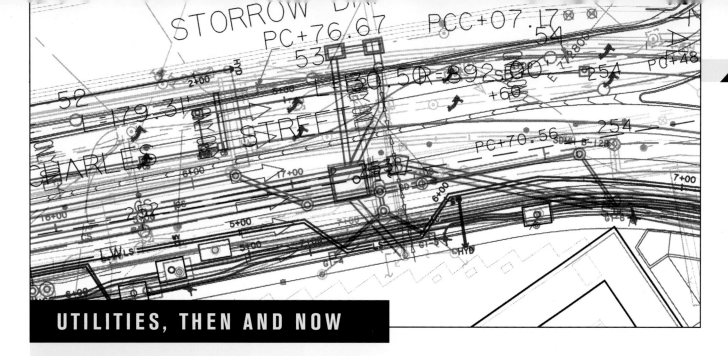

UTILITIES, THEN AND NOW

If utilities are a city's lifeblood, then by 1988 the city of Boston was ready for a heart attack. The ancient gas, water, sewer, telephone, electrical, and steam lines that run underneath the city's streets were ready to fall apart. The lines had been tangled around each other for over a hundred years, and untangling the mess took time and money. The Big Dig could not begin until every utility line was identified, unearthed, and relocated into new tunnels that would not be in the way of the construction. A utilities map (above) and photos from 1900 (below left) and 1999 (below right) illustrate the maze of utilities located under the streets of Boston.

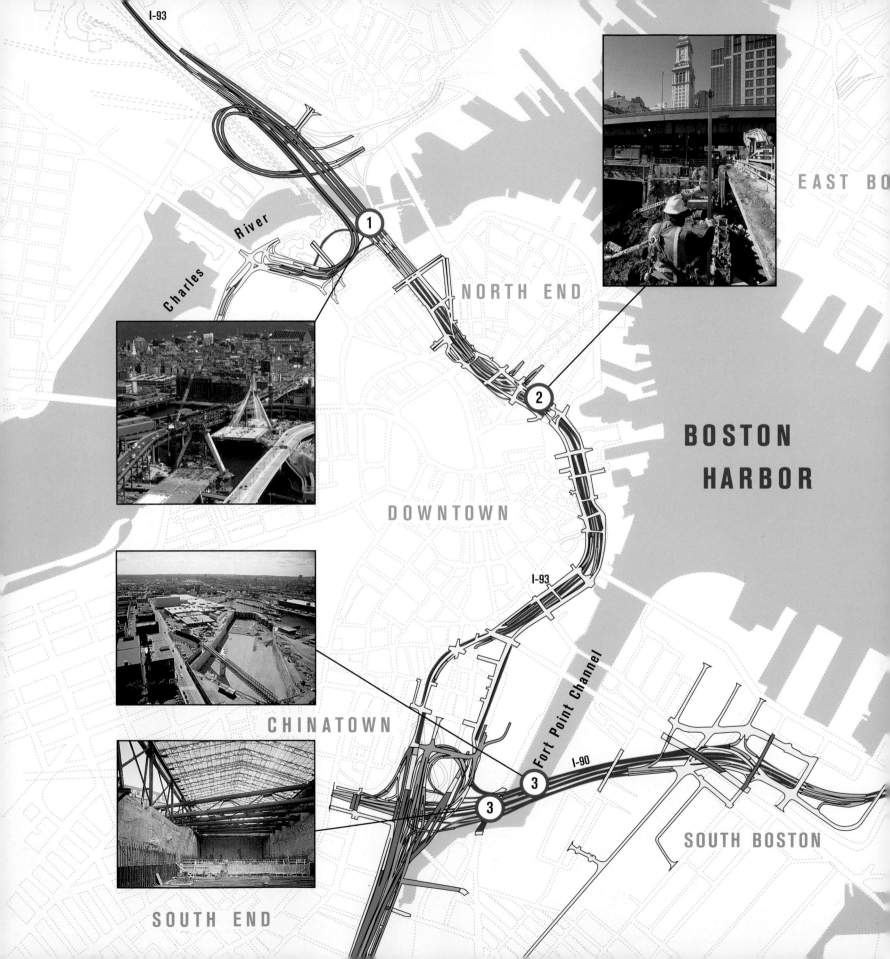

I-93

Charles River

NORTH END

EAST BO

BOSTON HARBOR

DOWNTOWN

1

2

I-93

CHINATOWN

Fort Point Channel

I-90

3

3

SOUTH BOSTON

SOUTH END

N

Ted Williams Tunnel

4

Logan
Airport

THE CENTRAL ARTERY/ TUNNEL PROJECT

The goal of the Central Artery/Tunnel Project is to improve Boston's network of highways so that traffic flows more smoothly in and around the city. This is being accomplished through four projects:

1. Replacing the decaying bridge over the Charles River with two new bridges, one of which is the widest cable-stayed bridge in the world.

2. Replacing the elevated, six-lane Central Artery (I-93) with an eight- to ten-lane tunnel running underneath the city.

3. Extending the Massachusetts Turnpike (I-90) into South Boston by building a tunnel underneath the Fort Point Channel.

4. Connecting Logan Airport to South Boston and the Massachusetts Turnpike by building a third tunnel under Boston Harbor.

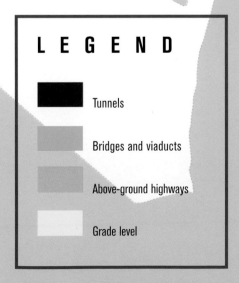

L E G E N D

Tunnels

Bridges and viaducts

Above-ground highways

Grade level

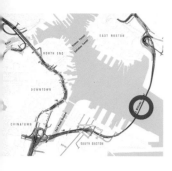

Under the Harbor:
The Ted Williams Tunnel

On December 19, 1991, a strange-looking barge moved slowly into Boston Harbor. Mounted on the barge was a huge machine called the Dutra Super Scoop, which began to take huge bites out of the bottom of the harbor—a process known as **dredging**. Over the next two years, the Super Scoop slowly ate its way across the harbor floor.

The job of the Super Scoop was to make a huge trench across the harbor that would act as an underwater cradle for a series of twelve immersed tunnel tube

The Dutra Super Scoop dredges mud and rock from the bottom of Boston Harbor. It took nearly two years for the Super Scoop to dig a trench connecting South Boston to East Boston.

sections, or ITTs. The ITTs would connect to form a tunnel between East Boston and South Boston. To dig the trench, the Super Scoop had to remove 890,000 cubic yards of rock and mud from the harbor floor. The finished trench was three-quarters of a mile long, 50 feet deep, and 100 feet wide.

BUILDING A BETTER TUNNEL ■ Digging the trench was the first step in building a four-lane tunnel underneath Boston Harbor to link the Massachusetts Turnpike with Logan Airport. Big Dig planners believed that connecting the turnpike to the airport would be one of the keys to alleviating traffic problems in Boston. Most of the cars bound for Logan Airport came from south and west of Boston and had to squeeze onto the Central Artery and through the crowded Callahan Tunnel to reach the airport. A new tunnel could divert this traffic away from the Central Artery and take it directly to the airport.

Although building a tunnel in Boston Harbor was nothing new, the methods used were. The first two automobile tunnels under Boston Harbor, the Sumner (built in 1934) and Callahan (built in 1961), were constructed by mining underneath the harbor floor and using a shield and compressed air to prevent the weight of the water from collapsing the tunnel. But building tunnels this way is dangerous and expensive. So Big Dig officials decided to use a safer and more economical method of tunnel construction: they would build the tunnel in sections, then place the sections carefully in a trench across the harbor floor.

Cars on the Central Artery head towards Logan Airport. Big Dig planners believe that the Ted Williams Tunnel will divert airport traffic away from the Central Artery.

FROM BALTIMORE TO BOSTON ■ While the Super Scoop was eating its way through Boston Harbor, steelworkers were constructing the steel tunnel sections in the Bethlehem Steel Shipyard in Baltimore, Maryland. Each tunnel section was big: 325 feet long, 40 feet high, and 80 feet wide—almost the size of a football field. Each ITT, looking like a set of giant binoculars, consisted of a pair of connected tubes (made of steel just 5/16 of an inch thick) that were sealed at both ends with steel plates, called **bulkheads**, to keep water out. Each tube was big enough to carry two lanes of traffic. When the first tunnel section arrived by barge in Boston Harbor

Tugboats help guide a steel tunnel section toward the Black Falcon Pier in South Boston.

on September 16, 1992, the city turned out its fire-boats to welcome the strange newcomer in style.

The first stop for the tunnel sections was the Black Falcon Pier in South Boston, where they were moored like gigantic submarines for outfitting. During the outfitting process, workers added concrete and steel reinforcing bar (rebar) to the inside of the tubes to create the foundation of the future four-lane roadway. As the concrete was poured into **forms** inside the steel tubes, they slowly sank in the water until they were just barely floating. Engineers had to be careful to balance the amount of concrete poured into the tubes—too much weight on one side would cause the ITTs to list like a stricken ship. It took five months to finish preliminary work on the first tunnel section, which weighed 33,000 tons (about half the weight of the *Titanic*) when the work was complete.

At the Black Falcon Pier, concrete pumps pour concrete into a steel tunnel section (below), causing it to sink. The concrete flowed into forms for the walls and the roadbed. To keep the tunnel tube level in the water, workers alternated the side into which the concrete was poured. After the concrete was poured, workers climbed inside the ITT (inset) to continue the outfitting process. Inside the tunnel, conduits for the tunnel's safety systems, electrical systems, and closed-circuit television cameras can be seen.

HOW TO DROP 33,000 TONS ON A DIME ■ Placing the completed tube sections in the trench dug by the Super Scoop required a huge boat, called a lay barge, that straddled each ITT like a pair of pontoons. Together they eased out into the middle of the harbor, where the barge gently lowered the huge tunnel sections into the trench. Maneuvering such a large object was a delicate and challenging process. There was no room for mistakes. With the assistance of lasers, the lay barge placed each tunnel section precisely next to the preceding tube.

Straddling a tunnel section that is attached by cables, a catamaran lay barge moves out into Boston Harbor. Each ITT was encased with so much concrete that, if the cables were cut, the tunnel tube would sink to the bottom.

Ten-foot-long horn beams at the ends of each tube fit into corresponding holes on the adjacent tubes, aligning them exactly. Giant rubber **gaskets** placed at the connecting points prevented water from getting inside the tunnel.

The ITT placed closest to the shore was outfitted with a snorkel, a steel shaft that stuck out of the water. The snorkel enabled workers and equipment to be lowered inside the tunnel and provided a supply of fresh air. Once inside the first tube, welders were able to begin cutting away the steel bulkheads sealing off each tunnel section while other workers resumed working on the roadway.

A CLEAN, DRY PLACE TO WORK ■

After the twelve ITTs had been placed in their trench at the bottom of the harbor and joined to each other, the underwater sections of the tunnel had to be connected with the land-side tunnel. To make a dry place to work, contractors built a giant concrete **cofferdam**, 250 feet across and 85 feet deep, at the edge of the harbor in South Boston. The cofferdam, which acted like a watertight fence, looked like a huge can shoved into the ground. At the bottom of the coffer-dam, workers joined the underground highway route from South Boston to the immersed tubes coming in from the harbor floor. Meanwhile, in East Boston, workers built a smaller coffer-dam to connect the other end of the immersed tunnel with a land-side tunnel leading directly to the airport.

The final work on the tunnel included installing lighting, signage, and ventilation equipment and placing more than a million tiles on the walls of the new tunnel. Two huge ventilation buildings were constructed at either end of the tunnel to pump in fresh air and pull out automobile exhaust fumes. When the tunnel was completed, state officials decided to name it after Boston Red Sox baseball legend Ted Williams. The Ted Williams Tunnel opened on December 15, 1995.

At the cofferdam in South Boston, the largest circular cofferdam in North America, workers connect the under-water section of the tunnel with the land-side section. The walls of the cofferdam were thirteen feet thick.

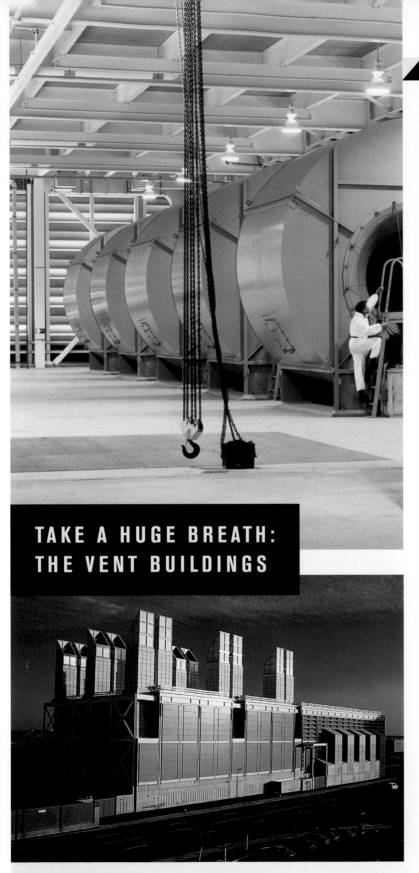

TAKE A HUGE BREATH: THE VENT BUILDINGS

No one wants to be trapped in a tunnel during a fire. Smoke and heat can build up quickly in such a tight space. But proper ventilation within tunnels can minimize the danger of a fire. With tunnels being such a major part of the project, Big Dig engineers had to design a way to get fresh air into their new tunnels in the event of such a disaster. To find a solution, they lit fires inside an abandoned tunnel in West Virginia and then measured the volume of air needed to pull fresh air into the tunnel and push out the smoke.

The fire tests helped Big Dig engineers create a sophisticated ventilation system that will not only save lives in the case of fire but also help improve the environment within the city. The ventilation system is housed in a series of handsome buildings built to express what they do—move air. Huge fans (above) force fresh air into the tunnels and suck automobile exhaust out of them. Distinctive stacks expel stale air and automobile exhaust high into the atmosphere.

Eight of these ventilation buildings have been built at different sites in Boston during the Big Dig, and each one is unique. Vent Building 7 (left), which ventilates the Ted Williams Tunnel, won the Harleston Parker Medal for architectural excellence.

OVER A SUBWAY
AND UNDER A RAILROAD

In the murky water of the Fort Point Channel in South Boston, huge concrete tunnel boxes sank gently into place over a subway tunnel. Meanwhile, two hundred yards to the west, **hydraulic jacks** shoved more concrete tunnel boxes underneath busy railroad tracks. Tunneling under railroad tracks and over a subway tunnel were all part of one of the most complex sections of the Big Dig.

This overhead view shows the wide array of construction that went on in South Boston. The tunnel that connects the Massachusetts Turnpike to the Ted Williams Tunnel runs diagonally underneath the railroad tracks in the foreground and continues through the Fort Point Channel, the adjacent body of water.

WHY A TUNNEL ACROSS THE FORT POINT CHANNEL? ■

Early in the planning stages of the Big Dig, no one could figure a way to connect the Massachusetts Turnpike to the Ted Williams Tunnel without relocating homes and businesses in South Boston. Then, one day in 1987, Bill Reynolds was standing at the edge of the Fort Point Channel, looking east. He could see a clear path across South Boston to Logan Airport, where a highway could go without demolishing any neighbor-hoods. So he called Fred Salvucci and said, "Fred, get down here. You have to see this. I just figured out your project."

Although Reynolds' route was a good one, the engineering would prove daunting. The Fort Point Channel once led to South Bay, a huge basin used by ships serving industries in Boston. Since the South Bay has been completely filled in, ships no longer pass through the channel. Today, artists, businesspeople, and razor blade manufacturers live and work in the area. What's left of the Fort Point Channel lies right at the end of the Massachusetts Turnpike, directly above a subway line, and next to Boston's busiest railroad station.

Workers put the finishing touches on a concrete tunnel box in the casting basin. The tunnel sections built for the Fort Point Channel crossing were 30 feet tall and weighed between 30,000 and 50,000 tons.

How do you construct an eight-lane highway through this complex place? First, you have to figure out how to build a tunnel underneath a series of busy railroad tracks and over a subway tunnel—two important transportation lines that cannot be disrupted. In addition, you must find a way to strengthen the weak soil in this part of Boston, which makes it difficult to build large, heavy structures.

BUILDING AN UNDERWATER BRIDGE ■ Big Dig engineers wanted to cross the Fort Point Channel the same way they had built the Ted Williams Tunnel, by floating tunnel sections into place with barges. But there was a problem: the bridges over Fort Point Channel are too low to allow the giant tunnel boxes to pass through. So they had to build a tunnel factory right in Boston. They called it the **casting basin**, and it was really big: 1,000 feet long, 300 feet wide, and 60 feet deep. It provided a clean, dry area to build tunnel boxes.

The Fort Point Channel tunnel passes directly over the eighty-five-year-old Red Line subway tunnel that runs down the center of the channel. Because the soil underneath the channel is weak, the heavy tunnel could easily have crushed the subway line. So the engineers had to figure out a way to shift the weight away from the Red Line tunnel. Their solution was to make an underwater bridge. Mike Bertoulin, a milestone manager for the Central Artery/Tunnel Project, explains: "First, we strengthened the soil on the western shore of the channel with a substance called soilcrete. The soilcrete was made by using huge drills, called soil **augers**, to dig

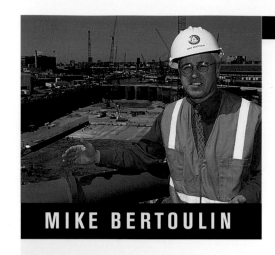

MIKE BERTOULIN

Mike Bertoulin is a milestone manager for the Central Artery/Tunnel Project. Mike's responsibility is to keep the extension of the Massachusetts Turnpike on schedule. That means he is in constant contact with engineers, designers, and contractors, figuring out ways to avoid setbacks and keep the project running smoothly. As a milestone manager, Mike gets to witness a lot of interesting discoveries. "Our workers are always bumping into old foundations and pilings that formed the old waterfront. It makes our work slow, but I get excited when we come across an old piece of timber from the 1800s. I know someone used these wharves long ago."

down about 125 feet to **bedrock**.
As the augers drilled, cement and
water were mixed into the soil.
When the mixture cured, the soil
was three hundred times stronger
than the weak clay under the
channel. Then, on top of the
bedrock underneath the channel,
workers built a bunch of solid
concrete legs to support the
tunnel sections. Since the tunnel
sections together weigh over
250,000 tons, they knew they
would need a lot of legs. To be
safe, they built 110."

When it came time to place the
completed tunnel boxes on the
support legs, workers flooded
the casting basin with water from
the channel. The tunnel boxes,
which were sealed at both ends,
floated to the top. Then **winches**
along the edge of the casting
basin carefully pulled the tunnel
boxes into the channel with cables. Once in position,
the tunnel boxes were submerged onto the huge underwater legs straddling the Red Line subway tunnel. The
legs fitted neatly into notches on the bottom of the
tunnel boxes, just like giant Lego blocks. Like the Ted
Williams Tunnel, each tunnel box had to be aligned and
connected exactly with the adjacent section.

*Big enough to hold an aircraft carrier,
the casting basin (top) in South
Boston provided a dry place for the
construction of tunnel boxes (above).
At the far end of the basin, a series of
round metal cofferdams filled with
crushed stone sealed out the water of
the Fort Point Channel.*

The flooded casting basin at night. The basin was flooded by removing the gravel from the cofferdams and pulling away the metal retaining walls.

The tunnel boxes didn't float right away because they were equipped with wooden ballast tanks that were full of water. Once the water was pumped out of the tanks, the tunnel boxes rose to the surface. To submerge the boxes, workers pumped water back into the ballast tanks.

PUSHING TUNNELS UNDER A BUSY RAILROAD ■

The other part of the Massachusetts Turnpike extension lies just west of the Fort Point Channel, where a series of railroad tracks carry thousands of commuters to and from Boston's South Station every day. Big Dig engineers had to figure out a way to construct the turnpike extension without shutting down these tracks.

Workers in the jacking pit construct the floor and walls of a tunnel box that will be pushed into place underneath a series of railroad tracks.

To construct a tunnel under a working railroad, workers had to build tunnel boxes in a huge pit and shove them under the railroad tracks—a process called tunnel jacking. The huge pit was known as the jacking pit, and it was similar to the casting basin. Workers constructed concrete tunnel boxes here, then pushed the boxes underneath the railroad tracks with very strong hydraulic jacks.

The weak soil underneath the railroad tracks, like that in the Fort Point Channel, had to be strengthened to prevent the tracks from collapsing into the opening at the end of the tunnel. Since there wasn't enough space to make soilcrete here, workers had to strengthen the soil by freezing it the way they freeze the ice on a hockey rink: by pumping brine (very cold salt water) through thin pipes drilled fifty feet down into the ground. Because frozen soil is much stronger than regular soil, the trains passed overhead without a problem. "Not one of the 65,000 daily commuters riding the railroad could feel all this construction going on only twenty feet below them," says Mike.

Digging out the frozen soil and pushing each tunnel box into place was a slow and difficult task. "We tried to get one good push a day. It took almost all day to dig three feet of frozen soil away from the front of the tunnel box," Mike explains. "We did this using a machine called a road header, which is like a dentist's drill, only a thousand times bigger. Once the road header digs three feet in front of the tunnel box, the hydraulic jacks go to work. Each jack can push about eight hundred tons, and it takes twenty of them all pushing at once to move a tunnel box." When the tunnel boxes were jacked exactly into place, they were connected with the tunnel tubes in the Fort Point Channel to form a single tunnel.

When this section of the Big Dig is finished, the Massachusetts Turnpike will connect to the Ted Williams Tunnel, enabling traffic bound for the airport to bypass the Central Artery and downtown Boston completely.

Tunnel Jacking

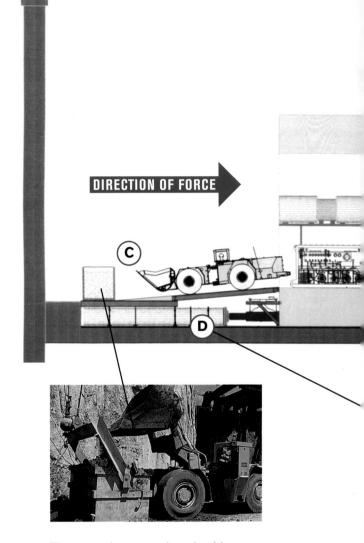

DIRECTION OF FORCE

The tunnel connecting the Massachusetts Turnpike to the Fort Point Channel tunnel passes underneath an active commuter railroad. A process known as tunnel jacking allows workers to build this tunnel without disturbing the railroad tracks.

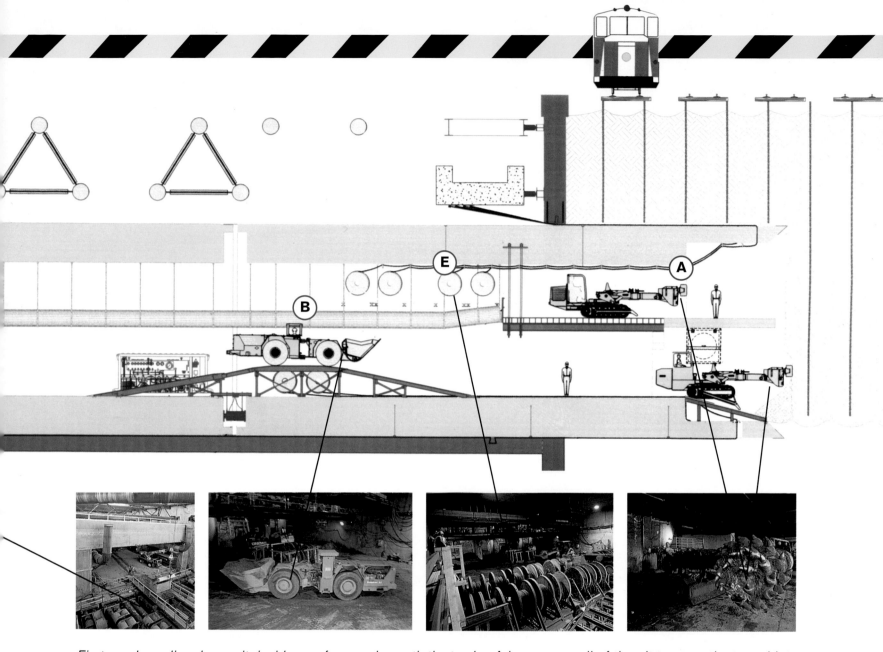

First, workers dig a large pit, inside of which they construct tunnel boxes of concrete and steel. The roofs of the tunnel boxes are extra thick, so that they can support the tracks above them once in place. When the tunnel boxes are finished, road headers **(A)** dig out the frozen soil from underneath the tracks. A low-profile loader **(B)** then takes the soil to the end of the jacking pit, where it is dumped into a bucket **(C)** and hauled out by a crane. Once three feet of frozen soil is removed, the hydraulic jacks **(D)** at the rear of the tunnel box push against the back wall of the pit to move the tunnel into the empty space. Greased steel cables fed from large spools **(E)** run on top of and underneath the tunnel box to make it easier to push into place. Then the digging starts again. It takes eight hours for a tunnel box to move three feet.

Within almost every concrete wall, ceiling, and road built for the Big Dig is a grid of steel known as rebar, which is short for reinforcing bar. On its own, concrete cannot withstand vibrations or any other forces that might cause bending. These forces cause concrete to crack. Rebar makes concrete walls stronger by giving them flexibility,

REBAR CONSTRUCTION

which enables them to absorb bending forces. The amount of reinforcing steel used in the Big Dig could make a one-inch bar long enough to wrap around the earth at the equator.

Janice Allen, one of the many women who work on the Big Dig, spends a lot of time working with rebar. "My work is not always easy, but it is important that it be done right. I like to think that the whole project will stand up strong because I have tied the reinforcing steel together correctly. I know it will all be covered up, but I am proud that my work is going to be a part of the city for a long time," she says.

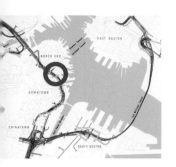

UNDER THE CITY: BUILDING THE NEW CENTRAL ARTERY

Excavators prepare the path of the new tunnel as traffic runs along the Central Artery above. The elevated highway sits on temporary underpinning. Just below the beams, at lower left, runs the Blue Line subway tunnel.

Downtown Boston is a sea of activity. Cars and trucks inch along the Central Artery during rush hour. Beneath the elevated highway, pedestrians and motorists work their way around detours and construction barriers. Meanwhile, below the streets, construction workers lay down the foundation for the new Central Artery, an eight- to ten-lane expressway that travels the same route as the old road, only underground. People who live and work in downtown Boston have grumbled about all the work going on, but it could have been much worse.

How do you build a tunnel directly beneath the streets and buildings of a busy and crowded city without shutting down the city? This was the question facing Big Dig engineers and designers. In the past, most tunnel construction in cities was done using a method known as cut and cover, where machines dig a large open trench while workers inside the trench construct the floor, walls, and roof

of the tunnel, then cover it with fill. But this method would not work in modern-day Boston because it would have required tearing down the Central Artery and closing off many streets, bringing the city to a near standstill. Engineers needed to figure out how to build a new Central Artery while keeping the old one, and the city, open for business.

BETH BOWER

John Carnes, a pewterer (metalworker) who lived in Boston during the 1700s, was a rich man. He imported wine from England and had the bottle caps stamped with his own name. We know this because he threw some of these caps into Mill Pond (in what is now the North End) in 1730. Beth Bower, an archaeologist, discovered these caps (above) 260 years later, right under the Central Artery. She did the digging in 1989, before any construction began on the Central Artery/Tunnel Project.

All federally funded construction projects are required by the National Historic Preservation Act to preserve the cultural resources at sites affected by the project. For the archaeologists working on the Big Dig, this meant mapping and excavating four sites in Boston noted for their potential historic value. The result has been a treasure chest of material providing a window into Boston's past.

Archaeologists learn about the past by carefully sifting through the layers of earth and garbage that have accumulated over centuries. On Spectacle Island in Boston Harbor, digging revealed an old pile of shells, or midden, left by Indians as long ago as 500 A.D. In two piles of this "trash," archaeologists found stone tools, harpoons, and animal bones, items that tell about the diet and lifestyle of the Indians who used them. At the Mill Pond site, archaeologists found tobacco-pipe stems, tin-glazed cups, and bowls made in Holland—telltale signs of colonial settlement.

Beth Bower notes that such discoveries are an unexpected and valuable result of the Big Dig. "We didn't know exactly what we'd find, but we would have lost these items forever without making the effort."

SLURRY WALLS ■ To solve this problem, Big Dig engineers and designers looked to Europe. Since the 1960s, underground construction projects in European cities—which are older and even more densely settled than Boston—have used slurry walls, which allows construction to go on beneath busy streets without too much disruption. Without slurry wall technology, the Central Artery/Tunnel Project would have been impossible. Slurry walls have enabled the construction of a tunnel under the city without disrupting the flow of traffic on the Central Artery.

A slurry wall is a concrete wall extending from the surface of the ground down to bedrock. To build the slurry walls for the Big Dig, construction workers dug a series of three-feet-wide by ten-feet-long trenches underneath and along each side of the Central Artery. The trenches run the whole length of the elevated road. To keep the trenches from collapsing, special machines pumped in slurry, a very dense mixture of clay and water that maintains pressure on the walls. With the slurry keeping the trenches intact, workers lowered steel beams into each trench to provide

Ironworkers install cross bracing on ceiling beams over the new Central Artery tunnel. This work was performed directly beneath the elevated highway and right next to historic buildings.

reinforcement, then filled the trenches with concrete, which displaced the slurry. The displaced slurry was pumped back into tanks to be cleaned and used again. When the concrete dried, it formed a strong wall.

The side-by-side slurry walls act like the walls of a house, which bear the weight of the roof. In this case, however, the roof is an elevated highway and the busy streets of downtown Boston. Once the slurry walls were complete, workers began excavating the dirt between them. Then they inserted steel beams, called struts, between the walls. Concrete decking strong enough to hold cars and trucks went on top of the struts to form a roof. The decking allows cars and people to go about their business above ground while workers and machinery complete the **excavation** and build the new tunnel directly beneath them.

This clamshell excavator (above) was used to dig the trenches for each panel of slurry wall. The slurry walls behind this worker (left) extend 120 feet up to the street. Cross-lot struts serve as braces to counter the weight of the city above.

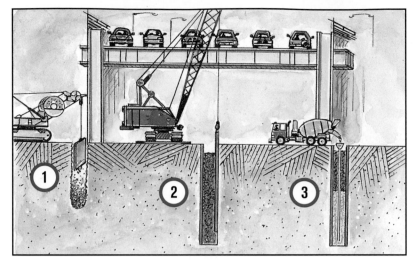

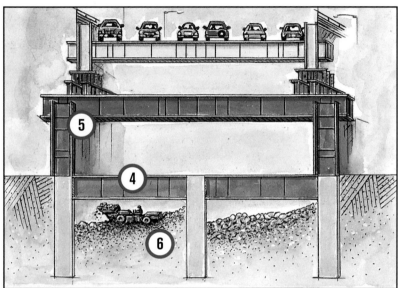

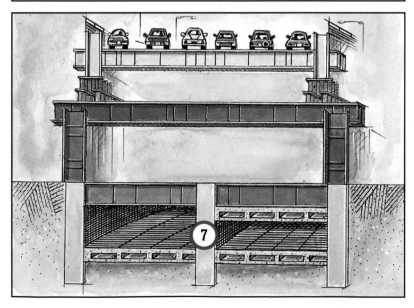

Slurry wall construction allows workers to excavate tunnels underneath the existing elevated Central Artery without having to divert traffic. In the first stage of the process (1), a clamshell digger digs a three-by-ten-foot trench all the way down to bedrock. The slurry is then pumped into the trench (2) to keep the sides from caving in and a steel beam is added for reinforcement. Finally, a concrete mixer pumps concrete into the trench, displacing the slurry (3). When the concrete cures, the wall can bear tremendous weight. A series of these sections forms one long slurry wall.

In order to support the elevated highway, workers build three parallel slurry walls through downtown Boston. Once the walls are finished, large steel beams are set between them and decking is placed on top (4). Then, on top of the decking and the slurry walls, workers construct steel underpinning (5) directly beneath the elevated highway. Workers then transfer the weight of the road to the underpinning and cut away the highway's old supports. Traffic flows continuously during this process.

After the decking has been laid down and the new supports have been put in place, tunnel excavation begins (6). Once enough earth has been removed, workers start building the road and constructing the tunnel that is to carry traffic under the city (7).

HOLDING UP A HIGHWAY ■

One of the most important jobs of the slurry walls is to support the old Central Artery during the construction. The elevated highway's original supporting columns rested on foundations that were directly in the path of the new tunnel. Because these foundations and columns needed to be removed, workers built a steel framework, called underpinning, directly on top of the slurry walls. Then the entire weight of the old Central Artery was transferred from the old supports onto the new steel underpinning. Once the weight of the roadway was transferred to the new supports, the old ones were cut away.

When this part of the Big Dig is completed, the elevated Central Artery will have been replaced by a wider underground expressway. Eventually, the elevated highway will be torn down, and the city will convert the land into parks and public space.

The red steel beams that support the elevated highway rest directly on top of the slurry walls. The struts at the bottom keep the slurry walls from collapsing inward as excavation progresses.

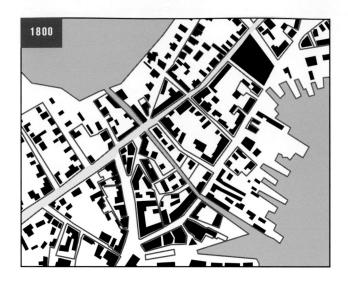

In 1800, Boston was a city of narrow streets, small houses, and shops. Hanover Street (in yellow) linked the North End to the rest of Boston. The creek running under Hanover Street connected Mill Pond with Boston Harbor.

By 1900, Boston had gotten bigger and more crowded. Houses, shops, and offices filled the downtown blocks. Hanover Street remained an important thoroughfare.

Downtown Boston in the year 2000. Where historic blocks and squares once stood, the Central Artery (in green) now dominates the landscape, cutting Hanover Street in half and breaking the link between the North End and the rest of the city.

This proposal for the year 2010 illustrates what the Central Artery corridor might look like when the Big Dig is done. The elevated highway is gone, and new buildings, parks, and streets knit the city back together. Hanover Street again connects the city to the North End.

HAYMARKET:
TEAMWORK FOR GOOD DESIGN

Highway projects in a large city require more than just figuring out how to connect roads. They require teamwork among all the people who have a stake in making a city work properly and look nice. A close look at just one block of the Central Artery/Tunnel Project—Parcel 7—demonstrates the teamwork required for good urban design.

"We knew the [Central Artery] tunnel needed a large vent building somewhere in the middle of town, to bring in fresh air," says Skip Smallridge, an architect who worked on the project. "We looked at ten locations and finally settled on Parcel 7 because we had enough room there to build and it would be less disruptive to residents in the nearby North End. We felt strongly that having a mixed-use structure would make for a better building, and we had many functions to squeeze into this one-acre parcel: a large vent building, a new subway entrance, a parking garage, retail shopping space, and an office building."

Designing this type of structure proved difficult. Skip explains: "Our vent stacks needed to be tall so that automobile exhaust would flow away from the city, but our building might then block the view of one of Boston's best landmarks—Old North Church. So we moved our vents away from the view corridor and wrapped our office building around the stacks to hide them. Finally, we also had to pay attention to our neighbors. The Blackstone Block nextdoor is one of the oldest intact blocks in the city, and is on the National Register of Historic Places. So our new building needed to reflect the character of this old block."

The work on the vent building called for cooperation among a variety of groups. "Our team included the City of Boston, the State of Massachusetts, the Environmental Protection Agency, the North End Residents Association, the Massachusetts Highway Department, and the Boston Landmarks Commission," says Skip.

OUT OF A TUNNEL
AND OVER THE RIVER:
THE CHARLES RIVER CROSSING

At the northern edge of downtown Boston a beautiful new cable-stayed bridge rises into the sky. Its towers echo the nearby Bunker Hill Monument, which commemorates a famous battle of the American Revolution. Its gleaming steel cables look like the rigging of a sailboat, in honor of Boston's maritime heritage. This is the Charles River Bridge.

Since 1955, cars and trucks traveling to and from the Central Artery have crossed the Charles River on the double-decked High Bridge. But, like the Central Artery, the High Bridge is an old and decaying structure that can no longer carry all the automobiles trying to use it. The new Charles River Bridge will take its place.

So many roads cross the river here at the northern edge of the city that the design of the bridge took several years. More than thirty different schemes were studied before a plan was selected. The final design called for a bridge unlike any other in Boston, one that would become an architectural landmark for the city. The new bridge starts at Causeway Street, where cars exit the underground Central Artery, and it will carry traffic across the Charles River and on to connections with Interstate 93 to New Hampshire.

Using a similar design, these young people are demonstrating how the new Charles River Bridge works. The forces that make this structure work are tension and compression. Their legs and torsos, like the towers of the bridge, are in compression, supporting the ropes that run over their shoulders. The ropes, like the bridge cables, are in tension, supporting the main span and the back spans of the bridge. The entire structure is balanced, stable, and economical.

HANGING TEN LANES OF TRAFFIC IN THE AIR ■ The Charles River Bridge is a cable-stayed suspension bridge. Two huge towers support a ten-lane roadway 1,457 feet long, weighing 100,000 tons—without traffic on it. Steel cables anchored in the two towers carry the weight of the roadway and the cars on it. The towers stand on strong legs that extend down to bedrock nearly a hundred feet under the river floor. The bridge is asymmetrical: eight lanes of highway travel through the legs of the towers, while two extra lanes hang off the east side of the bridge.

Kirk Elwell is the lead engineer on the bridge. It is his job to make sure the bridge is built the way engineers designed it. Kirk can provide some interesting details

The unfinished main span of the bridge hangs over the Charles River, held in place by the main span cables. With ten lanes of roadway, the Charles River Bridge is the widest cable-stayed bridge in the world.

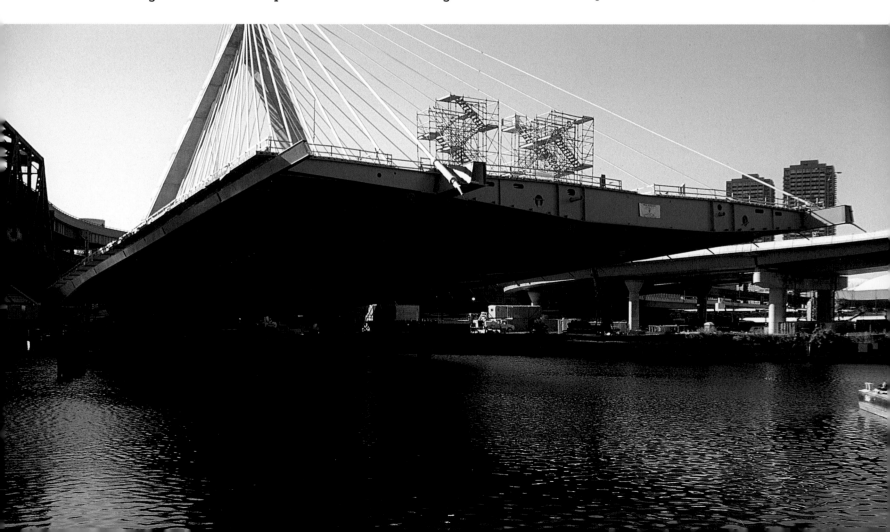

about the bridge. "We made the bridge out of both steel and concrete—the steel cables are in tension, and the concrete is in compression. Although many bridge towers are made of steel, we've used concrete for some good reasons. Concrete is an easy material to build with and is very strong in compression. Also, concrete does not require as much maintenance as steel, because it does not rust."

The first parts of the bridge to be built were the towers and the back spans, which anchor the structure to land. The hollow bridge towers are 270 feet high. Hollow towers are flexible, which allows the entire bridge to adjust as the loads on it change. They are also lighter than solid towers, which saves on foundation costs. Engineers were able to bend the bases of the towers inward to keep them away from the Orange Line subway tunnel, which runs under the Charles River and beneath the bridge.

"It took a crew of only twenty-four workers to build each tower: eight carpenters, eight ironworkers, four

The south tower of the bridge under construction. Steel falsework and plywood work platforms gave ironworkers and carpenters a sturdy, safe place to work. In the foreground, white cable anchors built into the back span are ready to receive cable strands from the tower.

field engineers, two crane operators, and two electricians," says Kirk. "We had two huge cranes that lifted concrete and steel up to the workers, and our crane operators could place three tons of steel delicately on a bridge deck 150 feet in the air."

Once the towers and the back spans were constructed, work on the main span over the river began. The main span was built in sections. To construct this part of the bridge, large cranes set on barges in the river lifted 130-foot steel girders up to a crew of ironworkers on the deck. The girders were held temporarily until cables from the towers could be anchored to their

An overhead view of a busy section of the Charles River. From left to right are the Charlestown Bridge, the Charles River Dam, the High Bridge, the new Charles River Bridge, The Leverett Circle Connector, and the Boston and Maine commuter rail tracks.

edges, supporting them permanently. Then the cranes placed lightweight concrete panels on top of the girders to form the roadway. As workers added sections of the main span to each tower, the gap between the two towers closed. Eventually, the two sides of the main span met in the center.

MUSCLES OF STEEL ■ While the towers and the spans form the skeleton of the bridge, the cables act as the muscles. Anchored in the towers, the cables carry the weight of the main span and the

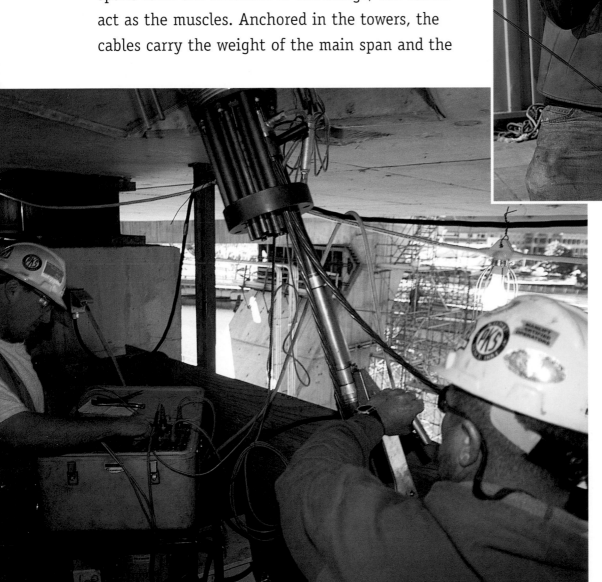

Cable tensioning begins when one strand (above) is attached to a pulley that takes it up to be anchored in one of the towers. Once all the strands in a cable are anchored above, engineers begin tensioning below. Tensioning is performed with a hand-held jack (left). An engineer watches a computer until the tension in each cable strand reaches exactly 30,000 pounds. The circular collar at the end of the jack distributes the same tension to all the cable strands as each one is pulled.

back spans. Each cable is made up of strands of wire rope that are only three-quarters of an inch thick, but tremendously strong.

To attach the cables from the towers to the bridge spans, workers pulled each strand of cable through a polyethylene sleeve. Then, in a process called tensioning, workers underneath the spans tightened each cable strand with a small electric jack. When all the strands in a cable were tightened, workers pushed a strong wedge against the whole cable to permanently anchor it to the span.

Tensioning each cable individually allowed engineers to balance forces in the bridge perfectly, like tuning a violin. Each cable takes a different load, based on which part of the bridge it is supporting and the angle it makes with the tower. The cables with the

most work to do are those that hold up the center of the main span, which is so far away. Each has seventy-three strands of wire rope, while those close to the towers have only fourteen strands each.

The new Charles River Bridge will be a distinctive Boston landmark for years to come. To complement this bold new structure, architects and artists are working to create a series of parks and art projects underneath the bridge. These improvements will provide access to a long-forgotten yet important stretch of the Charles River.

(Opposite) Twenty strands of steel form the cable inside this white polyethylene cable cover. The cable cover, or sleeve, protects the cable strands from cold and moisture.

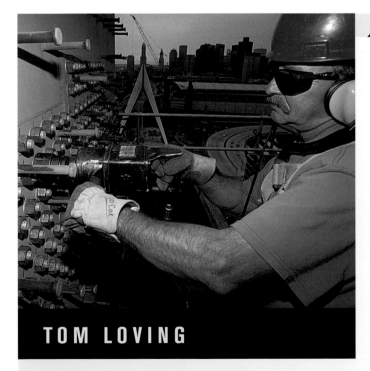

TOM LOVING

Tom Loving is an ironworker with Local 7, and he works for Kiewit Construction. One of Tom's duties was the "bolt up" of a steel anchor box at the top of the north tower of the Charles River Bridge.

The steel anchor box is a key component of the bridge. Every cable that enters the anchor box pulls with a force of 270,000 pounds. Without the steel anchor box, the cables would pull the concrete tower apart. The bolt up took about two days, and each bolt had to be tightened equally so that the anchor box acted as a structural unit.

Because Tom was exposed to the elements on top of the tower, making sure that everything was done safely was quite difficult. "It is noisy and windy and slippery up here. Safety is a really big problem," Tom says. Fortunately for Tom, the people who manage the Big Dig pride themselves on their attention to safety. For such a large construction project, the Big Dig has a remarkably low injury rate.

MITIGATION

Rebecca's staff found solutions to two of the biggest issues—noise and dirt. They promised that there would be no construction at night, and that crews would keep construction areas clean.

But mitigation is about more than just making the construction tolerable for the city's residents. It's also about making the city of Boston a better place to live. One goal of the mitigation effort is the creation of new parkland around the city. Spectacle Island, which was most recently a landfill for the city's garbage, is one of the spots that is benefiting from this effort.

"Look, we are going to dig a gigantic tunnel next to your home. There will be pile drivers, excavators, concrete trucks, temporary roads, and twenty-four hour shifts for a while—about eight years. Is this okay with you?" asked Rebecca Barnes in countless community meetings. Rebecca was in charge of urban design for the Big Dig, and she and her staff had a tough job.

The community meetings were part of a process known as mitigation. When cities undertake large construction projects, certain neighborhoods are negatively affected. Mitigation is the process of minimizing the impact, so that the quality of life in the affected neighborhoods is not destroyed. Through the process of mitigation, residents of these neighborhoods can voice their concerns about the project. After hundreds of community meetings,

Spectacle Island is becoming a public park: dirt and clay excavated from Big Dig work sites is being used to cap the unclean landfill so that the island can be developed for recreational use.

Another area benefiting is the land under the new Charles River Bridge. This land has been called "the lost half mile" of the Charles River. It was home to industries and railroads in the 1800s, but for years has been almost impossible to get to on foot. As part of its mitigation program, the Central Artery/Tunnel Project is enhancing the area with green space and public art. Ross Miller is one of the artists whose work will appear under the bridge. "Putting art under a highway bridge may seem strange, but I think this is a dramatic site and I hope my work will help people imagine what used to be here," he says.

(Opposite page, top) Because much of the work on the Big Dig is taking place within a dense city, project officials have gone to great lengths to make life bearable for the city's residents.

(Opposite page, center) Rebecca Barnes was an important figure in the mitigation process.

(Opposite page, bottom) Previously the site of a hospital, a resort, a horse rendering plant, and a garbage dump, Spectacle Island has been turned into a 100-acre public park.

(Above) Artist Ross Miller with some of his artwork.

(Left) Plans for the restoration of land along the Charles River.

Maintaining and updating the infrastructure

of big cities is complicated and expensive, but it is also important and valuable. Cities are exciting places that offer people many choices in a small area—choices of jobs, housing, education, and entertainment. Yet if cars choke the streets of a city, choices become limited and the quality of life declines.

Keeping our cities from being overrun by automobiles is a problem that will continue to plague us, unless cities are willing to make the best possible decisions about transportation. Not everyone thinks that building bigger highways is the solution to traffic problems, because it's expensive and time-consuming and highways already take up too much space in our crowded cities. Some feel that it would be cheaper and easier to fix our current highways. Others feel that cities like Boston should invest more money in public transportation, so that people don't have to drive as much.

Even though it has its critics, the Big Dig is the most innovative attempt to prevent cars from choking Boston's streets, and it is making the city a better place. For Boston, replacing a fifty-year-old elevated highway with a new tunnel under the city is more than a highway project. It is an effort to fix the problems

created by earlier generations. It is also the biggest improvement to the city in a century. Unlike most urban highway projects, which often create walls that separate one neighborhood from another, this project will knit together the fabric of a 370-year-old city.

Making huge changes to cities takes courage, compromise, imagination, and persistence. It is not easy, but when it is successful, it creates better places to live for every citizen. What could be more important?

G L O S S A R Y

AUGER: a large drill used to dig holes in soft soil. As it rotates, the auger fills with soil, which the device's rotating motion lifts to the surface.

BEDROCK: the solid layer of rock beneath the earth's surface. Buildings and other large structures built on bedrock have a solid foundation.

BULKHEAD: a temporary wall that separates one section of a structure from another.

CASTING BASIN: a large, dry area built for the construction of ships or other large structures.

COFFERDAM: a watertight enclosure out of which water is pumped to create a dry area for construction.

CONTRACTOR: a company that performs the work on a construction project.

DREDGING: the process of scooping up and removing mud and rock from the bed of a harbor.

EXCAVATION: the process of removing soil. Construction workers excavate so they can build tunnels or foundations; archaeologists excavate areas in their search for relics of the past.

EXPRESSWAY: a divided highway for high-speed through traffic; access is controlled by on- and off-ramps.

FORM: a mold in which concrete is placed to set. The form defines the final shape of the structure.

GASKET: a seal or buffer placed between two adjacent sections of a tunnel to prevent water from entering.

HYDRAULIC JACK: a device that uses pressurized water to exert force.

PENINSULA: an extension of land surrounded by water on three sides.

TURNPIKE: a road or highway for which tolls are collected.

WINCH: a powerful machine that moves large objects by winding up cable that is attached to the objects.

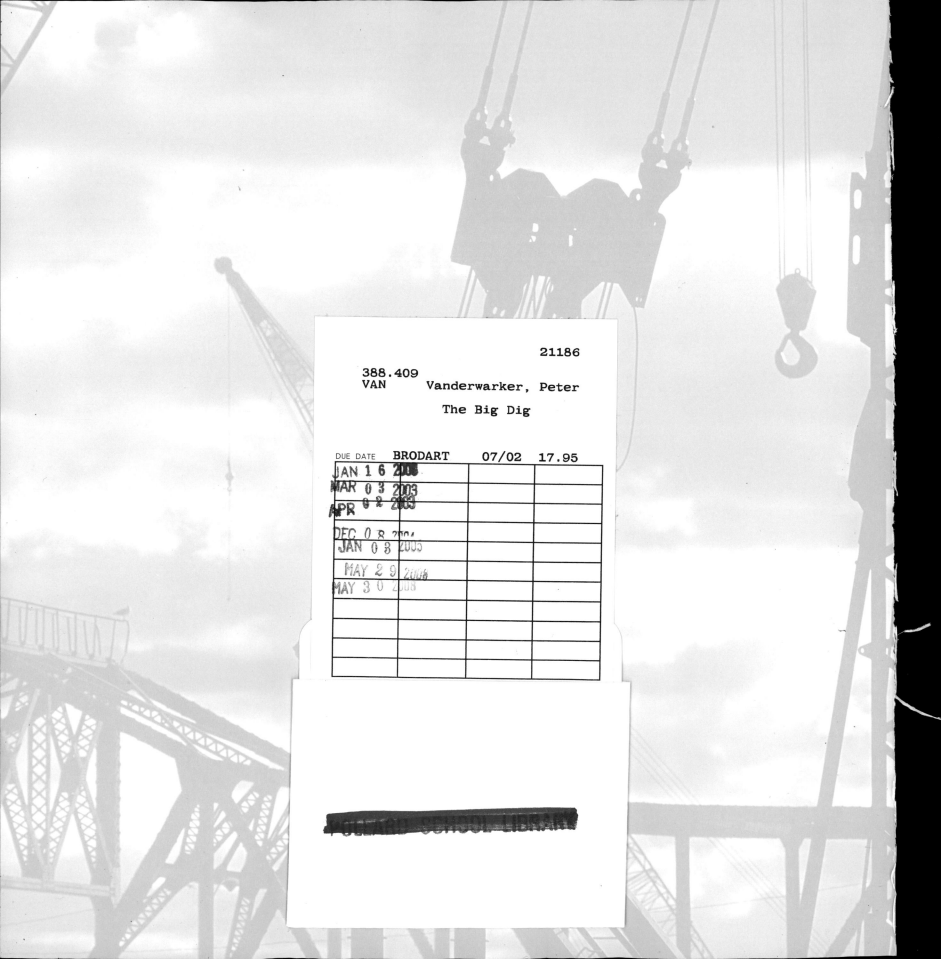